THE
WATER
BOOK

THE
WATER
BOOK

A USER'S GUIDE TO UNDERSTANDING, PROTECTING,
AND PRESERVING EARTH'S MOST PRECIOUS RESOURCE

The Water Book
Text copyright © 2011 Hatherleigh Press

Hatherleigh Press is a member of the Publishers Earth Alliance,
committed to preserving and protecting the natural resources
of the planet while developing a sustainable business model for
the book publishing industry.

This book was edited and designed in the village of Hobart,
New York. Hobart is a community that has embraced books
and publishing as a component of its livelihood. There are
several unique bookstores in the village. For more information,
please visit www.hobartbookvillage.com.

www.hatherleighpress.com

Library of Congress Cataloging-in-Publication Data is available
upon request.
ISBN: 978-1-57826-345-5

All Hatherleigh Press titles are available for bulk purchase,
special promotions, and premiums. For information about
reselling and special purchase opportunities, please call 1-800-
528-2550 and ask for the Special Sales Manager.

Cover Design by DCDESIGN
Interior Design by DCDESIGN

10 9 8 7 6 5 4 3 2 1
Printed in the United States

This book is dedicated to the Cousteau legacy.

Water is the principle, or the element, of things.
All things are water.

—PLUTARCH

CONTENTS

Part IV: What We Can Do to Create
A Sustainable Water Future

PUBLISHER'S NOTE

WATER IS in my blood. Three generations ago, my great-grandfather, Patrick McGovern, was tasked with the seemingly impossible: bringing fresh water from the great upstate watersheds to the growing metropolis of New York City. In an engineering feat, McGovern and his workers dug seventeen miles underground through mud and rock to construct what was at the time the world's longest single continuous tunnel. My great grandfather's aqueduct still serves the needs of the New York metropolitan area.

As I write this I am sitting in our offices in Hobart, in the center of the very same upstate watershed that drains into the great tunnel my ancestor built. Living in a watershed region has brought me greater awareness of the history of modern water use and its impact on communities, as well as the pressing need to preserve and protect our vital headwaters and sources. It has also made me conscious of the challenge of living and working in a region that is dominated by the water needs of a faraway city. Water is the vital link between country and city, between Hobart and New York City. Water connects us.

For too long we have taken the abundance of our water supply for granted without considering the alternative—namely, life without a seemingly endless supply of fresh water. The emphasis here is on "seemingly"; we have awakened as if from a dream to confront a planet that is on the verge of complete environmental collapse. We have awakened to a nightmare.

We are at a turning point in our planet's history. The choices we make today will affect the tomorrows of generations to come. Understanding our connectedness to water and the water cycle is at the core of those choices. Water fills our oceans, our skies, our veins. We must acknowledge that it is the essential task of humanity to be stewards of the Earth and guardians of its precious water.

—ANDREW FLACH, PUBLISHER

WATER SURROUNDS us. Falling from the sky, collecting in lakes and rivers and streams, quenching our thirst, nourishing our food sources— water is the critical building block of life. Known as the "Blue Planet", about 70% of Earth's surface is covered with water. With this finite resource being so fundamental to our survival, one must wonder why so many of us don't even know where our water comes from.

The Water Book provides a comprehensive look at why water is so important, an overview of the dangers our water supplies currently face, and what we can do in our daily lives to help ensure clean, safe water for the future.

The Water Book is simple and easy to read, inspiring and informative. Readers will be guided and empowered to make changes in their own lives to help preserve and protect Earth's precious water supplies.

—ALEXANDRA COUSTEAU

INTRODUCTION

W E ARE water people living on a water planet. More than half of Earth's surface is covered with water. The human body consists of more than 50 percent water.

Water surrounds us. It falls from the sky; it collects in oceans, lakes, rivers, and streams; quenches our thirst; nourishes our food sources. Water is the foundation of our existence—and our survival. Without water, our planet could not support life.

As incredible as it may sound, the amount of water on the planet hasn't changed since the earth's formation millions of years ago. It may appear that water comes from new sources, but in fact water is constantly changing form: after it comes down from the sky, water collects on the surface and goes underground, then eventually evaporates back into the clouds. Water is a constantly shifting supply.

Between Earth and its atmosphere, the amount of water remains constant; there is never a drop more, never a drop less. This is a story of circular infinity, of a planet birthing itself.

—LINDA HOGAN

The cyclical nature of water requires that we must understand the preciousness of this finite supply, value our relationship to its very essence, and take appropriate action to guard the purity of water at every stage so that fresh, clean water is abundant for generations to come.

As the world's population continues to increase, protecting our water supply becomes ever more important and even more challenging. The United Nations predicts that by 2025 close to two-thirds of the world's population (which already is nearing 7 billion) will face moderate to severe water shortages and the absence of clean water.

Pollution, sewage and industrial waste, and agricultural run-off all plague clean water sources and threaten the health of all living things. Climate change further contributes to the challenge by affecting the water cycle and causing droughts, floods, and changes to Earth's patterns of weather and temperature.

It is not too late for us to make a change. Individuals, communities, organizations, and nations are making efforts to help ensure that a healthy and stable supply of water is available in the future.

We forget that the water cycle and the life cycle
are one.
   —Jacques Cousteau

The first and most fundamental step is obtaining knowledge. The Water Book was created to provide you with an understanding of the intricacies of our planet's ecosystems, the fragility of its water resources, and how our lifestyle choices are truly endangering our clean water supply. We must identify and acknowledge the water connection on which we depend.

The second step is to see where we have gone wrong in our use and misuse of water resources. There is no one to blame. It is our hindsight that provides the understanding.

The final step is to realize that choices can be made. Each and every one of us can make a difference by changing our behaviors. Together we can have a significant, positive impact on the future of our precious water planet.

Some say that access to clean water is a human right. Rather than a right, consider this: it is a human responsibility to preserve and protect our water resources for the health of *all* life on the Blue Planet.

PART I
WATER,
SOURCE OF LIFE

THE MIRACLE
THAT IS WATER

Water is a truly miraculous resource. Water is all around us, falling from the sky and gathering in lakes and rivers, nurturing the earth and making life possible.

WHAT IS WATER?

Water is a small molecule made up of two hydrogen atoms and one oxygen atom. It is a clear, odorless, and tasteless element that can both absorb and hold heat, and it has the ability to take the shape of a solid, liquid, or a gas. Water is most dense at 39°F (4°C), when its molecules are tightly packed, although it freezes at 32°F (0°C; for saltwater to freeze, an even lower temperature is required). Water is an amazing

Thousands have lived without love, but not one has lived without water.
—W.H. AUDEN

element. With the presence of water on Earth, our planet became the only one in the solar system to support life. Our ecosystem was able to thrive because all the essentials necessary for life were there: energy (sunlight or chemical energy), temperature, atmosphere, gravity, nutrients, ultraviolet solar radiation protection, and water.

WHERE DID WATER COME FROM?

Water is believed to have first appeared on Earth during the planet's formation some 4 billion years ago. There are many theories about how water actually materialized and collected on Earth's surface. Some scientists believe it came from a small portion of the rocky material that made up the surface, and others conjecture that volcanic activity was responsible for releasing water into the atmosphere. There is also a theory that ultraviolet rays broke apart water and hydrogen molecules in the atmosphere, and another theory that suggests comets with a composition similar to Earth's had collided with our planet, bringing it water.

Run-off: *noun*
: precipitation water drained by streams and rivers

Water in the oceans has played a critical role in the evolution of life on Earth. Although there is much debate over exactly how life began, it is generally accepted that life on Earth was limited to unicellular (single-celled) organisms until 610 million years ago, when multicellular organisms appeared in the ocean. From these humble beginnings, life-forms ranging from sponges and algae to slime molds began to evolve. Over the next 100 million years, plants and fungi began to grow on land. Animals and insects soon followed, and later, human beings. In more ways than one, we are beings born of water. In fact, each one of us begins life in the water environment of the womb. We are truly water people living on a water planet.

THE WATER CYCLE

Water exists because of a precise, delicate cycle. Although there is no exact beginning or end to the cycle, we can start by understanding water evaporation. The cycle begins when water evaporates. Water evaporates in two ways. The first is by the release of water from lakes, rivers, and oceans into the air. The second is when water evaporates through plants in a process called *transpiration*. During transpiration,

Evaporation: *noun*
: the change of a liquid into a vapor at a temperature below the boiling point

plants draw water from the soil and release it back into the air. About 10 percent of the moisture in the atmosphere is a result of transpiration; the rest is the result of evaporation from oceans, lakes, streams, and other bodies of water.

In the next stage of the cycle, evaporated water condenses in the air and falls over the land and waterways in the form of precipitation. The amount of rainfall received globally can range from 0.1 inch per year in some desert regions to over 900 inches per year in the tropics. This precipitation is soaked up by plants and collects in lakes, river, and oceans. Then, plants and other bodies of water release water into the air through evaporation/transpiration, and the cycle repeats itself. The water cycle keeps the planet's water supply continuously moving and transforming from one form to another.

WE NEED WATER TO SURVIVE

Human beings can't survive without water. Plants and animals, life-forms great and small, all depend upon the existence of water for their survival. Water is critical to sustain life.

Humans can only consume *freshwater*, which is

Transpiration: *noun*
: the passage of watery vapor through the skin
or through any membrane or pore

defined as water that has a salt content of less than
.1 percent. By contrast, seawater consists of approximately 3.5 percent dissolved salts. Although we need
salt to live, saltwater contains an extremely high
amount of sodium, much more than our bodies can
handle. Consuming saltwater will lead to dehydration
faster than not drinking any saltwater at all because
in an effort to dilute the high salt content, the water
molecules already present in our cells will abandon
their normal function, and our bodies will gradually
shut down.

We rely on freshwater for daily survival. A woman
typically needs about 0.7 gallons (2.7 liters) of water
per day, and a man needs closer to one gallon (3.7 liters). Often, humans are advised to drink eight glasses
of water per day to replenish the body's water supply,
but food provides about 20 percent of our daily water
needs; beverages such as milk or juice also provide
hydration. We also need water to support and sustain
our food supply. Animals and crops require fresh,
clean water to produce the resources necessary to feed
the planet's billions of people.

Condensation: *noun*

: the act or process of reducing a gas or vapor to a liquid or solid form

THE LIMITS OF FRESH WATER

Our freshwater supplies are severely limited. Although over half the planet is covered in water (about 70 percent), close to 97 percent of this is saltwater; therefore, only 3 percent of our planet's water supply is suitable for human consumption. It is possible to remove salt to make saltwater suitable for human consumption through a process called *desalinization*, but this costs around five times as much as processing freshwater. Of the small quantity of freshwater suitable for consumption, about two-thirds of that is unavailable because it is trapped in ice. Thus, the drinking water we can use comes from two places: *surface water* (lakes and rivers) and *groundwater* (water from wells). Groundwater is a source of water that we cannot see. This underground water supply exists as soil moisture and in *aquifers* (layers of permeable underground rock, sand, silt, gravel, or clay containing water that can be extracted using a water well).

While almost 10,000 cubic miles (over 400,000 cubic kilometers) of water flow from Earth's rivers into the seas, some scientists believe there is actually more

Precipitation: *noun*
: a form of water, such as rain, snow, or sleet, that condenses from the atmosphere, becomes too heavy to remain suspended, and falls to the Earth's surface

water trapped in the planet's mantle than the amount held in all the oceans.

THE WONDER OF WATER

The following chapters feature more about the wonder that is water and explain how water sustains everything we do, from eating to drinking to producing everyday goods. It is our responsibility to guard this important resource for the future.

2

OCEANS:

OUR PLANET'S WATER WORLD

The wonder of water is present in the oceans. Life began in the oceans, and today countless animals, plants, and fish rely on these bodies of water. The world's oceans are amazing treasures that must be respected and protected.

OUR OCEANS are a world unto themselves, home to more than an estimated 1 million fascinating life forms (of which only around 200,000 are known to science). Blue-green algae was one of the first organisms on Earth, and today it is still an important part of the biosphere. Algae are part of a group of underwater plants that create the "forests of the sea," coral reefs. Coral reefs consist of acres of plant life that are critical

The oceans are the planet's last great living wilderness, man's only remaining frontier on earth, and perhaps his last chance to produce himself a rational species.

—JOHN L. CULLNEY

food sources for fish and other animals. The largest coral reef in the world spans over 1,200 miles, and the deepest part of the ocean stretches over 35,000 (over six miles) feet below sea level—a length that is greater than the height of Mount Everest, which stands at just over 29,000 feet (about five and a half miles). Although they in fact make up one massive body of water, the world's oceans are divided into five separate oceans: the Atlantic Ocean, the Pacific Ocean, the Indian Ocean, the Southern Ocean, and the Arctic Ocean.

THE WORLD'S OCEANS

The Atlantic Ocean, which includes several seas, among them the Caribbean Sea, the Mediterranean Sea, and the North Sea, covers approximately 20 percent of Earth. The portion of the Atlantic between Europe and North America was crossed by great explorers, which enabled the growth of Western civilization and, years later, provided a passageway for thousands of immigrants seeking a new home in the United States.

The Pacific Ocean is the largest of the five oceans and covers about one-third of Earth's surface. The Pacific contains approximately 25,000 islands, which is most of the world's islands; temperature in the ocean

Man is not an aquatic animal, but from the time we stand in youthful wonder beside a Spring brook till we sit in old age and watch the endless roll of the sea, we feel a strong kinship with the waters of this world.

—HAL BORLAND

ranges from freezing (near the poles) to 86°F. The Pacific is a source of many riches, including pearls, petroleum, and natural gas, but its greatest gift by far is its fish. Herring, salmon, sardines, tuna, and other fish, as well as shellfish, thrive in the Pacific.

The Indian Ocean is the third largest of the world's oceans. Although the Indian Ocean is affected by monsoon winds, it is generally calmer than the Atlantic or Pacific. Furthermore, the monsoon winds enabled sailing, which allowed the Indonesian peoples to settle in Madagascar and encouraged trade by sea far earlier than in the Atlantic and Pacific Oceans. Some of the world's earliest civilizations developed along rivers that are linked to the Indian Ocean. These include the people of ancient Egypt, who lived along the Nile, as well as those in Mesopotamia, who dwelled by the Tigris-Euphrates.

The Southern Ocean encircles Antarctica but it is not bordered by any land mass, so many consider it part of the Atlantic, Pacific, and Indian Oceans. The Southern Ocean is the "youngest" of the oceans. It formed about 30 million years ago when South America and Antarctica separated. A band of water unimpeded by any landmass, winds blow across the ocean all the way

I am miserable out of water. It is as though you had been introduced to heaven, and then found yourself back on earth. The spirituality of a man cannot be completely separated from the physical. But you have made a big step toward escape simply by lowering yourself under water.

—Jacques Cousteau

around the globe, causing large waves and dangerous conditions for ships. The Southern Ocean freezes and icebergs exist throughout the year.

The Arctic Ocean, located on the opposite side of the globe, is the smallest and shallowest of the five oceans. Much of the Arctic Ocean is covered by sea ice throughout the year, and in the winter it is almost entirely covered by ice. Petroleum and natural gas can be found in the Arctic Ocean, and some scientists estimate that it contains hidden oil and gas resources. Whales, walruses, and polar bears make their home in the water, on the ice, and along the coast of this ocean. Despite the brutal cold, this area of the world has a fragile ecosystem that does not adapt well to change and is slow to recover from harm or destruction.

THE ABUNDANCE OF OCEAN LIFE

Hundreds of thousands of life-forms, including fish, animals, and plants, call the ocean home. Over 200,000 different marine species live in the world's oceans, and every year scientists find more than 100 previously undiscovered species. Aquatic species have flourished in this great, wild space for millions of years. Our oceans are truly incredible frontiers.

3

LAKES, RIVERS, AND STREAMS:

ARTERIES OF THE EARTH

In addition to the wonder of the oceans, our Earth's rivers, lakes, and streams have shaped the land and fostered animal and plant life on its shores. These bodies of water are some of our greatest treasures.

RIVERS, LAKES, and streams color Earth's surface, thriving everywhere from dense forests to seemingly barren deserts. These great bodies of water have endured through the millennia.

When you put your hand in a flowing stream, you touch the last that has gone before and the first of what is still to come.

—LEONARDO DA VINCI

MIGHTY RIVERS

Rivers shape the landscape of glaciers, mountains, and plains all around the world. Rivers flow towards oceans, lakes, seas, or other rivers; depending on their size, these bodies of water are also referred to as streams, creeks, or brooks. Rivers can consist of either saltwater or freshwater and are largely kept flowing due to surface *runoff*—a result of precipitation falling to the ground and flowing into lakes and rivers. *Groundwater seepage* is another source of water for rivers. This occurs when a river infiltrates an area of land with a very high concentration of water. The river then begins to draw water from the water-rich environment.

Some rivers form deltas where they empty. These deltas occur when a river carrying sediment reaches a standing body of water. Sediment gradually builds up and widens the river. Seen from space, the branches of a delta can resemble the shape of a triangle, flower, or tracks of a bird's footprint. The Nile River forms a lotus-shaped delta where it drains into the Mediterranean Sea. This river delta is one of the largest in the world, spreading over 200 kilometers (approximately

A lake is the landscape's most beautiful and expressive feature. It is earth's eye; looking into which the beholder measures the depth of his own nature.

—HENRY DAVID THOREAU

124 miles) of coastline. Several hundred thousand water birds make their home in the Nile's delta, as well as hundreds of species of animals and fish.

Perhaps the best-known delta in the United States is that of the mighty Mississippi River. With its headwaters in Minnesota, the Mississippi meets with the Ohio and Missouri rivers before flowing into the Gulf of Mexico. It is here, as the Mississippi flows into the Gulf, that the delta has formed. Over the years, the delta has grown so large, partially a result of human manipulation of the river, that the state of Louisiana has advanced southward 15 to 50 miles into the gulf. At 2,350 miles long, the Mississippi is the longest river in the United States whose waters and delta provide some of the greatest concentration of marshland and fishery harvest in the country.

THE WORLD'S LAKES

There are also a number of important lakes throughout the world. In the United States, the Great Lakes—Lake Michigan, Lake Erie, Lake Superior, Lake Huron, and Lake Ontario—are so large and have such a wide variety of ecosystems that they are often considered to be "inland seas." The Great Lakes were created as a result

A river seems a magic thing. A magic, moving, living part of the very earth itself…for it is from the soil, both from its depth and from its surface, that a river has its beginning.

—LAURA GILPIN

of prehistoric glacial movement. These lakes support a fertile agricultural region along with impressive fisheries and a number of rare species, including populations of the white catspaw, pearly mussel, the cooper redhorse fish, and the Kirtland's warbler.

Each of the world's lakes has its own distinct characteristics, including the chemistry of the water, water level, and ecosystem. The Dead Sea, located in the Middle East, is actually a lake, and it is one of the world's most unique bodies of water. Bordered on the western edge by Israel and the West Bank and on the eastern edge by Jordan, the Dead Sea is the lowest lake in the world, sitting 1,385 feet (422 meters) below sea level. But what makes this lake so interesting is its incredibly high salt content. At approximately 33.7 percent salinity, the Dead Sea is one of the saltiest (hypersaline) lakes in the world, nearly nine times saltier than any of the world's oceans. It is known as the Dead Sea because the salt content makes it such a harsh environment that no life can be supported in its water.

Desalinization: *noun*
: the process of removing salt, especially from sea water so that it can be used for drinking or irrigation

VITALITY OF RIVERS AND LAKES

Earth's rivers and lakes are fascinating bodies of water, each unique in its own way. Life thrives on their banks and shores, and a wide variety of animals make their homes in those waters. Rivers and lakes nurture Earth and make life possible.

PART II
HUMAN WATER USE, PAST AND PRESENT

THE ROLE OF WATER IN HUMAN HISTORY

For millennia, water has made possible the growth of civilizations. Societies have thrived on the banks of fertile rivers, which provided a source of food as well as transportation. The history of cultures around the world is closely linked to the wonders of bodies of water.

S INCE THE formation of the earliest societies, ready access to a water source has influenced where people have chosen to settle. Fertile river valleys provided the resources necessary for successful agriculture. With agriculture and access to consistent food production, animal domestication became

Water is the only drink for a wise man.
—HENRY DAVID THOREAU

possible and more people could be fed on a regular basis. Villages grew into towns, towns into major cities, and civilizations boomed all around the world, from Mesopotamia and Egypt in the Middle East to Rome and North America.

TRANSPORTATION AND EXPLORATION

Another impetus to the development of civilization was the possibility for transportation provided by bodies of water. With the advancement of ship building, bodies of water played a crucial role in exploration and trade, cementing the might of history's greatest cultures. In the 16th century, Portuguese explorer Ferdinand Magellan travelled the globe for Spain. He was the first to sail from the Atlantic Ocean to the Pacific Ocean through what has since come to be known as the "Strait of Magellan," and it was his journey that began the Spanish quest to circumnavigate the globe, which was completed successfully in 1522. With a new westward route to Asia, Spain established territories abroad, expanded its power in Europe, and by the 17th century, controlled an empire larger than any before it. Exploration not only strengthened government, but

The frog does not
Drink up
The pond in which
He lives.
        —NATIVE AMERICAN
    PROVERB

it also brought new goods and cultures to European shores and fostered learning, growth in the arts and literature, and important scientific discoveries.

NATIVE AMERICAN FOLKLORE

In North America, water plays a pivotal role in the story of creation for many Native American tribes. Although tribal beliefs vary, one of the oldest and most common myths centers around the sea. In this myth, a water creature, such as a turtle or duck, swims to the bottom of the sea and returns with a lump of mud. This becomes Earth. Often, the Earth's land is supported on the back of a turtle. Water is held sacred in many Native American societies and is an important part of Native American ceremony.

SHAPING AMERICAN HISTORY

During the early years of European exploration of America, rivers were critical for travel along the East Coast and the goods proffered from these travels supported entire industries, such as the fur trade. The importance of bodies of water continued through the centuries.

Water, thou hast no taste, no color, no odor; canst not be defined, art relished while ever mysterious. Not necessary to life, but rather life itself, thou fillest us with a gratification that exceeds the delight of the senses.

—ANTOINE DE SAINT-EXUPERY

In the United States, bodies of water have inspired and nurtured generations of Americans. One great example is the Hudson River. Named for the Englishman Henry Hudson, who sailed for the Dutch East India Company in the 17th century, the importance of the Hudson River and the Hudson Valley continued to grow as America established herself along the East Coast. The Hudson Valley, which spans from New York City through upstate New York, was an area of major conflict during the American Revolution, when the British tried to split the colonies in two by taking over the river. Not long after America won the war, in 1781, a new century dawned and the invention of the steamboat made the Hudson a main line for industry as well as transportation for those who wished to escape the crowding of New York City. Industries thrived along its shorelines, and a series of towns and cities were established that are still prominent today. By the mid-1800s, the Hudson had also inspired the Hudson River School art movement, and years later in the 1970s, it was a driving force behind environmental regulation. The Hudson Valley has become an icon of American history and a hub for the arts as well as agriculture.

Aquifer: *noun*

: an underground layer of permeable rock, sediment (usually sand or gravel), or soil that yields water

The Mississippi River has served as a major commercial waterway for centuries, and its strategic location in military battles has cemented its place in history books. The Mississippi is also an important part of American folklore. Running from the northern United States all the way to the Gulf of Mexico, the miles of the Mississippi have come to symbolize a true American journey. Many authors have used the river as inspiration for their writing, most notably Mark Twain, who recounts the journey of Huck Finn and his journey along the Mississippi in *The Adventures of Huckleberry Finn*, a classic American novel about the search for freedom.

WATER IS OUR PAST AND OUR FUTURE

Throughout human history, water has provided us with nourishment, both physical and spiritual. Great bodies of water opened up pathways to new lands that brought new discoveries and new opportunities. Pivotal moments in history have taken place on the banks of rivers, lakes, and streams. Works of art and literature have been born in reflective waters both

We must begin thinking like a river if we are to leave a legacy of beauty and life for future generations.

—DAVID BROWER

calm and powerful. The gift of water is the birthright of future generations, and those of us who are here now are responsible for protecting our oceans, lakes, and rivers just as we would guard any other landmark or natural wonder.

WATER AND THE
WAY WE EAT

Each human being needs water in order to live, and water is also crucial to our food sources. The availability of freshwater ensures that we are able to put food on the table.

AROUND THE world, freshwater is essential to produce food for billions of people. Any farm requires water to grow grains, fruits, or vegetables. Whether we are growing crops for human consumption or to feed livestock, water ensures that we do not go hungry.

Many of us are unaware of how much water is required for a plant to grow from small seeds into

Water is the driver of Nature.
—LEONARDO DA VINCI

fruit-bearing trees, miles of grain, or a field of fresh vegetables. The amount of water required by a crop during a production period is its *water requirement*. Although water requirements vary depending upon the type of crop and the area where the crop is grown, water requirements are in general a lot higher than we think. According to the United States Geological Survey, it is estimated that a single meal of a simple salad and milk, for example, requires nearly 100 gallons of water: a single serving of lettuce requires 6 gallons of water; tomatoes require 3 gallons; and milk requires 65 gallons. Even a single serving of almonds requires 12 gallons of water.

DELIVERING WATER FOR OUR CROPS

Water is delivered to crops through a process called irrigation. Without *irrigation*, large-scale farming would be impossible and desert regions of the world would be without a food supply. The United States Geological Survey (USGS) estimates that almost 60 percent of the world's freshwater is used for irrigation. Central states primarily rely on groundwater for

We call upon the waters that rim the earth, horizon to horizon, that flow in our rivers and streams, that fall upon our gardens and fields, and we ask that they teach us and show us the way.

      —NATIVE AMERICAN,
        CHINOOK BLESSING LITANY

irrigation, while the western states typically use their surface water resources.

There are three main types of irrigation: *flood irrigation*, *center-pivot irrigation*, and *drip irrigation*. Flood irrigation has been the most commonly used process and simply requires the transport of water to a field, where the water is then directed to flow through crop areas. Center-pivot systems have also become popular, particularly in the Midwest. In center-pivot irrigation, sprinklers along a length of pipe are fed water from the center. The machine is mounted on wheels and moves in a circular pattern over several days. However, the drip irrigation system has distinguished itself as the most efficient system because it reduces water evaporation by one-fourth. Drip irrigation involves watering plants slowly, drop by drop. A network of valves and tubing equipped with drippers delivers water directly to the roots.

IRRIGATION AND SUSTAINABLE WATER SUPPLY

Using water for irrigation presents its own set of problems if the water is not used effectively. It is estimated that approximately 40 percent of water dedicated to

High-quality water is more than the dream of the conservationists, more than a political slogan; high-quality water, in the right quantity at the right place at the right time, is essential to health, recreation, and economic growth. Of all our planet's activities—geological movements, the reproduction and decay of biota, and even the disruptive propensities of certain species (elephants and humans come to mind)—no force is greater than the hydrologic cycle.

—EDMUND S. MUSKIE

global agriculture evaporates because of inefficient irrigation systems. This is particularly a problem in developing countries.

Although the ultimate goal is to utilize irrigation processes that are effective and sustainable, the United States has indeed seen a considerable increase in the amount of freshwater channeled for irrigation. In fact, withdrawals from lakes, rivers, reservoirs, and groundwater for irrigation increased by 68 percent from 1950 to 1980, but this number later stabilized from 1980 to 2000. The USGS attributes this stabilization to climate, crop type, advances in irrigation, and higher energy costs.

FEEDING FUTURE GENERATIONS

Today, the challenge is greater than ever to determine the best way to water our land for food while at the same time preserving the water cycle. Utilizing new drip irrigation technology provides us with one solution, but these methods must be used and monitored around the world to be effective. Freshwater is essential to provide us with nourishment, and it is only through effective use of this precious resource that we will be able to feed future generations.

PART III
HUMAN USE AND IMPACT ON WATER

6

REROUTING RIVERS AND LAKES

Our need for water to irrigate fields, provide energy, and supply us with drinking water means we often reroute rivers and lakes. This can have a devastating effect on ecosystems.

REROUTING LAKES for irrigation has consequences. Perhaps one of the world's best-known lakes is one that is rapidly disappearing. The Aral Sea, located in Central Asia between Kazakhstan and Uzbekistan, was one of the four largest lakes in the world before the Soviet Union began to divert its waters for irrigation projects in the 1960s. Since then, the Aral Sea has decreased to about 10 percent of its original

The permanence of our dams will merely impress the archaeologists; their numbers will leave them in awe. In this century, something like a quarter of a million have been built in the United States alone.

—MARK REISNER

size, thus destroying the region's previously prosperous fishing industry. Additionally, ever-increasing economic and environmental problems are creating a public health issue as the remainder of the sea has become seriously polluted.

THE USES AND IMPACTS OF DAMS

In the United States, rivers are often rerouted for irrigation as well as for energy. The Colorado River, which passes through a series of incredible landscapes, including the Grand Canyon and Arches National Park near Moab, Utah, is one example of a river shaped by several man-made dams. These dams make use of the river as a water supply for drinking and agriculture, as well as a source of energy.

Beginning just north of Great Lake, Colorado, the river originally flowed through the southwestern portion of the United States into northern Mexico and the Gulf of California, but it has since been modified by several powerful dams. Among the dams that sequester significant portions of the river's contents are the Glen Canyon and Hoover dams. Today, the Hoover Dam is a source of hydroelectric power for

Water is the basis of life and the blue arteries of the earth! Everything in the non-marine environment depends on freshwater to survive.

—Sandra Postel

the states of Nevada and Arizona as well as select cities in California, including Los Angeles. The state of Nevada receives nearly 2 percent of its electricity from the dam. The main purpose of rerouting the Colorado River, however, is to supply water for fields and crops. Nearly 90 percent of water allocated from the river is used for irrigation purposes. In the Southwest, where much of the land is dry desert, the Colorado River is crucial to sustain the lives of hundreds of thousands of people.

The largest generator of hydroelectric power in the world is the Three Gorges Dam along the Yangtze River in China. Completed in 2006, the dam is a feat of engineering, spanning over a mile and a half in width and rising to a height of more than 600 feet. The Three Gorges Dam brought major economical and social benefits to the region, allowing 10,000-ton ocean freighters to reach the interior of China for up to six months out of the year. Furthermore, the dam provides a huge source of energy to the country without releasing any emissions. Despite these benefits, the Three Gorges Dam has displaced over 1 million people, flooded archeological and cultural sites, increased the region's risk of landslides, and spread

Humans build their societies around consumption of fossil water long buried in the earth, and these societies, being based on temporary resources, face the problem of being temporary themselves.

—CHARLES BOWDEN

environmental toxins. During the dam's construc-
tion, factories, mines, waste dumps, and other areas
of industrial activity were flooded and forced under
water; now, pollutants from those areas linger in the
dam's reservoir, which stands hundreds of feet deep
and close to 400 miles long.

As seen with the Three Gorges Dam, although
dams can be critical to ensure a consistent supply of
energy and water for irrigation, their presence can
transform the ecology of an area and decimate the
natural functions of that environment. A dam essen-
tially splits a river in two, blocking water flow and any
natural ecosystem functions that would occur. Water
is held and released in unnatural ways, putting original
riverbanks under water and causing a drastic change
in flow downstream. Large sediments and debris are
trapped and build up in the reservoir, creating a faster
downstream flow and more quickly eroding riverbeds.
With no transport of sediments, the downstream area
is stripped and unable to support a habitat. Unless human assistance is provided, migratory fish have great
difficulty navigating a dammed river, and the survival
of sustainable fish populations is greatly reduced.

Delta: *noun*

: a nearly flat plain of alluvial deposit between diverging branches of the mouth of a river, often, though not necessarily, triangular

Dams can even cause deviations from normal oxygen and temperature levels, factors that threaten fish.

If dams are built correctly, however, and if effects on the ecosystem are carefully considered and problems are addressed, these man-made structures can provide a consistent energy supply and source of water for irrigation and at the same time allow for those important natural functions of the river. Although a dam is a solution that requires a manipulation of natural processes, extra care can ensure the longevity of the river.

USING TECHNOLOGY RESPONSIBLY

Dams should be acknowledged as powerful options for providing energy and sources of irrigation in situations where these resources may be desperately needed. Yet their possible dangers can't be ignored. Dams that cause environmental problems, such as China's Three Gorges Dam, should be carefully studied and analyzed so future projects can be improved. We should also be aware of how rerouting lakes effects our environment. Otherwise, long-standing environmental problems are a major risk.

WATER AND OUR HEALTH:

THE DANGERS
OF POLLUTION

In addition to climate change, pollutants also have dangerous effects on our Earth's bodies of water. Pollution threatens the beauty of our landscape as well as the lives of many animals, aquatic life, and plants.

OUR MODERN way of living is taxing the water supply in many ways. All around the world, pollution makes freshwater dangerous to drink, causes serious health problems, and affects the life cycle of fish, aquatic life, and plants—and, in turn, the health of humans that consume these food sources.

Filthy water cannot be washed.
—AFRICAN PROVERB

Pollution of waterways and a lack of sanitation are major threats to clean water and our health. Understanding how this occurs is the first step to initiating change. We need to learn to make better choices in order to protect the cleanliness of our water—and we must start today.

WHAT CAUSES WATER POLLUTION?

A 2005 national assessment of United States water quality performed by the Environmental Working Group showed that most of America's tap water—42 states collectively—contained the following:

- 83 agricultural pollutants
- 59 contaminants from sprawl, urban areas, or polluted runoff and wastewater treatment facilities
- 166 industrial chemicals (factory waste)
- 44 pollutants from by-products of water treatment or leaks from pipes or storage tanks

These forms of pollution have many sources. The first step towards making long-term changes and

If you could tomorrow morning make water clean in the world, you would have done, in one fell swoop, the best thing you could have done for improving human health by improving environmental quality.

—WILLIAM C. CLARK

protecting clean water for the future is understanding how pollution arrives in our water supply. Once we have an understanding of pollution and its repercussions for plants, animals, the planet, and all of us, we can act effectively and make improvement a reality.

AGRICULTURAL RUNOFF

Agricultural runoff is the result of by-products used in industrial farming, including chemical fertilizer and fecal matter from manure, that leak into the water supply. Two nutrients used in most synthetic fertilizer, nitrogen and phosphorus, are dangerous in large quantities. They can deplete oxygen in aquatic environments, such as streams, and cause harm to fish, plants, and other animals. Fecal bacteria from manure further pollutes the water, making it unsafe for human recreational use or drinking.

The result of pollution like this has far-reaching consequences. Many polluted rivers in the United States flow to the Gulf of Mexico, where the combined effects of hundreds of gallons of chemical nutrients causes the overgrowth of algae in an area known as the Dead Zone. Algae reduce oxygen levels in the water, which causes the death of plants and fish. This area

Water is fundamental for life and health. The human right to water is indispensable for leading a healthy life in human dignity. It is a pre-requisite to the realization of all other human rights.

—THE UNITED NATIONS COMMITTEE
ON ECONOMIC, CULTURAL AND
SOCIAL RIGHTS

of lifeless water, which is roughly 6,000 square miles, threatens the massive fishing industry supported by the gulf.

Additionally, states in our nation's Farm Belt area such as Illinois, Kansas, Missouri, and Indiana have been faced with water pollution caused by excessive use of pesticides that have leaked into city water supplies and become a likely cause of higher birth defect rates and fertility problems. Agricultural runoff is difficult to stop because it is often hard to trace the source of the pollution, as it is often caused by multiple farms. Left unregulated, factories and farms can take advantage of the convenience and low cost of dumping their waste into nearby waterways rather than properly dispose of the harsh chemicals that are used in manufacturing and food production.

CHEMICAL AND TOXIC WASTE

Chemical and toxic waste causes severe damage to our water supply, damage that can last years and have extensive consequences. Toxic chemicals in the air cause acid rain, a form of atmospheric pollution. Often, this acid rain is the result of coal-burning energy plants and waste incinerators. These sources release everything

Irrigation: *noun*
: the artificial application of water to land to assist in the production of crops

from harmful mercury to phosphorus and polychlorinated biphenyls (PCBs) into the air and, eventually, our water supply. Nuclear waste is another dangerous pollutant that is a by-product of radioactive materials used in industrial, medical, and scientific processes.

PHARMACEUTICALS

Within the past decade, scientists around the world have discovered evidence of pharmaceutical waste in water and soil. In 2002, the U. S. Geological Survey study discovered organic wastewater contaminants (OWCs), including chemicals from over-the-counter drugs and personal care products, in 80 percent of 139 streams sampled in 30 states.

Pharmaceutical chemicals enter the environment in one of two ways: through excretion when waste from humans or animals treated with drugs enters the waterways through the sewage system; or through disposal when unused, discarded drugs end up in a landfill or sewage system. After these drugs enter the waterways, water treatment plants attempt to eliminate them. However, most water treatment plants cannot fully eliminate these chemical compounds.

Although the long-term effects of pharmaceutical

Hydroelectric Power: *noun*
: a form of energy generated by the conversion
of free-falling water to electricity; the genera-
tion of electricity by using the motive power of
water; also called hydroelectricity

waste in drinking water and soil on humans is not yet known, scientists are already starting to link disturbing effects on fish and other wildlife to the presence of chemical waste in the water. Often, water tainted with pharmaceutical runoff results in the feminization of male fish, tumors, and reduced appetite.

Today, cities and towns are struggling to fix water that has been tainted with chemical waste. As the use of pharmaceuticals by the general population increases, we will struggle even more with the best way to dispose of unwanted drugs.

THE DEVASTATION OF OIL SPILLS

A recent example of toxic pollutants damaging our water systems is the BP oil spill, which occurred in the spring of 2010 off the coast of Louisiana. The BP oil spill has been referred to as the worst oil spill seen in the United States since the Exxon Valdez accident in 1989. On April 20, 2010, the drilling rig *Deepwater Horizons*, leased by BP, experienced an explosion in the Gulf of Mexico that set off a life-threatening fire. Two days later, at a location about 50 miles off the coast of Louisiana, the rig sank. Crude oil rushed from

Gray Water: *noun*
: dirty water from sinks, showers, bathtubs, washing machines, and the like, that can be recycled, as for use in flushing toilets

a broken pipe, releasing close to 1,000 barrels of oil a day below sea level. Capping the broken pipe proved to be a challenge; it took weeks to make substantial progress in sealing the pipe and collecting excess oil. Furthermore, over 400,000 gallons of dispersant (a polymer meant to dilute oil droplets) were applied to help control the spill—an amount that greatly exceeds what is usually applied to oil spills in the United States. The EPA was responsible for overseeing the dispersant application, measuring their toxicities and taking daily air and water quality samples to monitor the changes to the marine environment.

The repercussions of the spill were severe. Because it was an oil spill so close to the shoreline, scientists were concerned for the contamination of ecosystems like wetlands, which provide a habitat for a vast range of organisms including birds, fish, crabs, and grasses. In particular, biologists believe sea turtles may mistake the oil for clumps of grass and ingest the toxic substance. These marshes are important to humans as well, as they are a home for some of the country's most desired seafood. As of May 12, 2010, the deaths of 18 birds, 6 dolphins, and 87 sea turtles have been reported as possibly caused by the spill.

Watershed: *noun*
: the region or area drained by a river, stream,
etc.; drainage area

TRASH AND OUR WATERWAYS

A more common pollutant to our waterways is trash. When we throw something away, we may forget that our trash takes its own path to disposal. Currently, pollution is threatening the ocean and the fish, animals, and plants that call it home. An example of this is the Trash Vortex (also known as the Eastern Pacific Garbage Patch or the Asian Trash Trail) that has formed in the Pacific Ocean area between California and Hawaii. Ocean currents have picked up millions of tons of the world's discarded plastic and other trash, creating a trash dump that National Geographic has estimated is twice the size of Texas.

Very few are aware of the severity of the situation and the extreme ways in which plastics are polluting the ocean. At least 10 percent of the nearly 260 million tons of plastic produced this year are predicted to end up in trash vortices like that in the Pacific Ocean. Much of the plastic has been broken down into small pieces, thus contaminating the ecosystem and killing a significant amount of marine life. Efforts are now being made to help solve this problem, and increasing awareness is the best first step.

Aquaculture: *noun*
: the cultivation of aquatic animals and plants, especially fish, shellfish, and seaweed, in natural or controlled marine or freshwater environments; underwater agriculture

Bottled water production also takes a huge toll on the environment. For example, water packaged in Europe travels over 6,000 miles to get to California, a trip that wastes fuel and pollutes the environment. It is estimated that bottled water ends up as over 1 million tons of plastic trash every year. Over 45 million gallons of oil are required to produce the plastic for the bottles, and plastic's slow decay rate causes those water bottles to stay in the environment—often drifting in our oceans—long after they've been thrown away.

MAKING CHANGE A PRIORITY

In order for human beings to survive, we must have ready access to clean, drinkable water. Everyone—from politicians in the United States to people dwelling in rural villages, towns, and cities around the world—must actively look to improve the water supply. The planet's population is continuing to grow at a rapid pace, and with it so does the demand for a reliable, clean water supply.

8

WATER:

A DISRUPTED BALANCE

Water exists as part of a delicate balance. Disruption of this balance causes many global effects including changing sea levels, drought, endangered animal habitats, and a dwindling supply of clean water.

AROUND THE world, the balance of our water supply is being disrupted. This is causing threats to human life. Climate change caused by our modern way of living is having tremendous effects on the world's water, and repercussions like droughts and rising sea levels are the result. These frightening realities directly affect millions of people. Access to clean water is also out of balance. People in many parts of the world do not have a supply of safe water to drink.

In an age when man has forgotten his origins and is blind even to his most essential needs for survival, water along with other resources has become the victim of his indifference.

—RACHEL CARSON

If we neglect to monitor the effects of our way of living on the world's water supply, the result will be human lives at risk.

THE DISRUPTION CAUSED BY CLIMATE CHANGE

Through evaporation, condensation, and precipitation in the form of rainfall, the water cycle regulates the movement and distribution of the world's water. However, climate change is a powerful force, one that impacts the water cycle. This is leading to rising sea levels and an increase in droughts, crises that threaten human life.

Increases in human carbon emissions have altered world temperatures, disrupting the balance in our earth's environment all around the globe. As temperatures rise, we lose more water to evaporation and the natural balance of the water cycle is disrupted.

Temperature shifts have other dangerous effects on the world's water supply. Climate change is so powerful that it is having an effect in some of the coldest places on earth. As Arctic areas grow warmer, the ice caps begin to melt. For animals that live and hunt exclusively on ice (such as seals and polar bears), melting

Water flows from high in the mountains
Water runs deep in the Earth
Miraculously, water comes to us,
And sustains all life.
—THICH NHAT HANH

ice translates to shrinking habitats, which is leading to starvation for many animals. Melting ice caps and an increase in saltwater could also cause saltwater to be pushed into underground sources of freshwater. An increase in sea levels could displace approximately 75 percent of the worlds freshwater, a major consequence for life around the globe.

RISING SEA LEVELS

Rising sea levels threaten the lives and homes of thousands. In the Maldives, an archipelago of nearly 1,200 coral islands in the Indian Ocean, the rising sea levels put inhabitants in danger. The country lies just 4.9 feet (1.5 meters) above sea level, and the progression of climate change at its current pace would likely send the islands underwater in less than 100 years. As part of a course for action, the Maldives's president Mohamed Nasheed has appealed to the United Nations for global cuts in carbon emissions and has begun setting aside a portion of the country's tourism revenue for purchase of a new homeland for Maldives's 396,000 residents. Other options have included constructing dikes to hold back the waters and building the island upward. A wall has already been built around the capital city

I have said that I thought that if we could ever competitively, at a cheap rate, get fresh water from salt water, that it would be in the long-range interests of humanity which would really dwarf any other scientific accomplishments. I am hopeful that we will intensify our efforts in that area.

—JOHN F. KENNEDY

in hopes of protecting against tidal surges. However, these only provide short-term solutions.

It is certain that rising sea levels have severe consequences, and we must pay attention to what these changes tell us about climate change so we can take steps to prevent further damage.

FACING CHALLENGES OF DROUGHT

A rise in droughts linked to climate change is also reducing the water we need for our crops and, in turn, threatening our food supply and the livelihood of many.

According to the Environmental Protection Agency, there are a number of factors that connect climate change with a decline in agricultural productivity:

- average temperature increase
- change in rainfall amounts and patterns
- rising atmospheric concentrations of CO_2
- pollution levels such as tropospheric ozone
- change in climatic variability and extreme events

Aqueduct: *noun*
: a conduit used to convey water over a long distance, either by a tunnel or more usually by a bridge

Although temperature increases may actually provide a benefit to farmers by giving them a longer growing season, prolonged summer heat could also destroy crops as soil moisture evaporation rates increase, causing more frequent and severe droughts. In the United States, this is a particular concern for the Great Plains region as well as for growers of California wine grapes. In Australia, rice has been abandoned as a major export crop because of an intensive six-year drought. By 2008, Australian rice production had been reduced by 98 percent, and global prices for rice tripled that same year. Drought threatens the livelihood of many and has extensive repercussions.

OUT OF BALANCE: ACCESS TO CLEAN WATER

Today, the balance of the distribution of clean water around the world is compromised. Many developing nations don't have the resources available to create or enforce legislature pertaining to clean water, which makes access to clean water a matter of lack of infrastructure. Communities in sub-Saharan Africa and South Asia are at the greatest risk; without sanitation

Estuary: *noun*

: the wide lower course of a river where it flows
into the sea

facilities, these communities are unable to maintain good hygiene practices.

UNSAFE CONDITIONS

Consumption of unclean water leads to serious health problems, especially for children, who can contract life-threatening cases of diarrhea and malaria. Often, these diseases could easily be prevented if impoverished communities had proper sanitation. Sadly, unsafe water and unsanitary conditions cause 80 percent of disease around the world and cause tens of thousands of preventable deaths each year.

However, the reality beyond our backyard is that, according to the United Nations Development Programme, 1.2 billion people currently lack access to safe water. This translates to about one in eight people across the globe.

The United Nations Development Programme also reports that 2.6 billion lack access to basic sanitation. UNICEF has reported similar statistics, adding that over 884 million people still use unsafe water sources. Members of communities must expend enormous amounts of time and energy trekking several miles to draw water that often isn't even safe to drink. In Africa

Floodplain: *noun*
: a nearly flat plain along the course of a stream
or river that is naturally subject to flooding

alone, it is estimated that the cost of taking time to journey to water sources prevents economic growth and costs over 25 billion dollars. In many instances, women and children are responsible for this task; they walk long distances only to wait in a line of people whose need for water far exceeds what the well can provide. When children spend their day getting water, no time is left for them to attend school, and a cycle of poverty is initiated. If safe water were nearby, communities could spend valuable time and energy building a better way of life and educating their children.

MAKING CHANGES FOR THE FUTURE

Around the world, it is necessary to make conscious and voluntary efforts to preserve the delicate water cycle and ensure a lasting supply of clean freshwater for humans everywhere. Each one of us has a responsibility to slow the increase in global temperatures to halt climate change's effect on the world's water, and we must work to balance the distribution of clean water so all people on the planet use their right to its supply.

9

WHO OWNS
THE WATER?

*Clarifying who owns water is going to be key in ensuring
that people around the world have access to safe, clean
water. Making sure those who have access to clean water
sources act responsibly is an important issue.*

W HEN WE think of water use, we often don't
consider the water required to produce goods.
Below is a list of some commonly manufactured items
and the amount of water used in their production:

- 1 sheet of paper: 10 liters (approximately 3
  gallons)
- 1 orange: 50 liters (approximately 13 gallons)

When the well's dry, we know the worth of water.

—BENJAMIN FRANKLIN

- 1 slice of wheat bread: 40 liters (approximately 11 gallons)
- 1 cotton shirt: 2,700 liters (approximately 713 gallons)

The need for this much water to support our way of living means that water is in great demand.

WATER AS A COMMODITY

Today, water is considered a commodity to be bought, sold, and traded globally—a system known as *water privatization.*

The term water privatization includes a wide scope of objectives—water utility operations, management, and ownership arrangements. There are three main types of water privatization.

- Outsourcing is the private contracting for water utility plant operation and maintenance and private provision of services and supplies.
- Design, build and operate requires the negotiation of a contract with a private firm for the building and operation of new, expanded or updated facilities.

The crisis of our diminishing water resources is just as severe (if less obviously   immediate) as any wartime crisis we have ever faced. Our survival is just as much at stake as it was at the time of Pearl Harbor, or the Argonne, or Gettysburg, or Saratoga.

—JIM WRIGHT

- Asset sale is the government sale of water/waste-water assets to a private company.

(As adapted from State Environmental Resource Center)

Before World War II, nearly half of the United States' water systems were privately owned. When the Clean Water Act (the CWA, also known as the Federal Water Pollution Control Act), was passed in the early 1970s, a larger amount of government funding became available to support water-related projects.   As a result, municipalities had greater access to technology to upgrade treatment facilities, thus decreasing the number of privately owned water systems. However, the federal contribution to clean water has significantly fallen. Federal funds accounted for 78 percent of total clean water spending in 1978; in 2007, that contribution fell to a mere 3 percent. This has allowed private companies to again fill that void.

Geyser: *noun*

: a natural hot spring that regularly ejects a spray of steam and boiling water into the air

BOTTLED WATER AND OWNERSHIP OF WATER SUPPLIES

A good example of water privatization at work is in the case of bottled water companies. The bottled water industry has become a significant consumer of the global water supply.

This increase in water privatization causes issues across the globe. Because the quality of bottled water isn't regulated, many companies can sell bottled water that is the same, or very similar, to the quality of tap water. Furthermore, in some regions, companies have begun to dominate the clean water source, bottle it, and then sell it back to the people at higher prices. As a result, bottled water companies make access to clean, affordable water difficult for residents, oftentimes polluting and/or depleting any reliable local resources. With water privatization, local water infrastructure is also often forgotten and communities are left trying to create their own reliable water system and treatment facilities—a difficult and commonly unsuccessful task.

Hardness: *noun*

: the quality of water that causes it to impair the lathering of soap caused by the presence of certain calcium salts

CLEAN WATER FOR ALL

In understanding the problems that can result from water privatization, we must begin to recognize that water is not simply a commodity but is a necessary natural resource. Although water can certainly be bought and sold—on both the individual and communal levels—the importance of the resource must be attributed to its role as a building block of human life. Clean, affordable water must become internationally accessible and thus be included in the mission statement of companies privatizing water.

PART IV

WHAT WE CAN DO TO CREATE A SUSTAINABLE WATER FUTURE

10

PROTECTING
OUR WATER

*In the United States and around the world, efforts are
being made to clean up our water supplies and protect
them for the future. Governments are recognizing the
need for change in legislation, and improvements are
also taking place on a local level. One thing is clear:
no matter where it takes place, change begins with one
person and is strengthened as more individuals join in.*

THE NOTION of protecting water as a resource
is not new; in fact, water pollution issues were
first addressed by the United States government when
Congress passed the Rivers and Harbors Act of 1899.
Efforts to clean up water and ensure its cleanliness for

Plans to protect air and water, wilderness and wildlife are in fact plans to protect man.
—STEWART UDALL

the future began in earnest in the second half of the 20th century, when the Clean Water Act (CWA) was passed in 1972.

NATIONAL EFFORTS FOR CHANGE: PROTECTING AMERICA'S WATERWAYS

Prior to the CWA, many major waterways of the United States were in unfathomable decline. The Hudson River had bacteria levels 170 times the safe limit—so high that those exposed to the waters had to receive vaccinations to protect against the pollutants. The Cuyahoga River in Ohio actually caught fire in 1969, becoming the only waterway ever to be declared a fire hazard. Even the mighty Mississippi was feeling the effects of pollution. Raw sewage and industrial waste were being dumped in water systems and there were no effective means of controlling this pollution.

In 1972 the CWA was passed by Congress as a means of cleaning up the country's surface water. The United States Environmental Protection Agency (EPA) defines the CWA's objective as working "to restore and maintain the chemical, physical, and biological integ-

We think of our land and water and human resources not as static and sterile possessions but as life-giving assets to be directed by wise provisions for future days.

—FRANKLIN D. ROOSEVELT

rity of the nation's waters." This is done by controlling the types and amounts of pollution released into waterways as well as assisting facilities responsible for wastewater treatment. The act also strives to guard our water by "maintaining the integrity of wetlands" and supporting "the protection of fish, shellfish, and wildlife and recreation in and on the water."

LOCAL EFFORTS FOR CHANGE

As expected, much of the responsibility for cleaning and protecting waterways falls to residents in the area who value their local water resources the most. Legislation and protection acts filed by the EPA have been successful in restoring and protecting waterways, but perhaps the action with the greatest impact is that taken by local residents and organizations.

In the Greater Boston region, a number of organizations dedicated to environmental and river issues join together each Earth Day to clean up the 80 miles of the Charles River. The event has been going on for eleven years and in the spring of 2010 drew in 3,600 volunteers (www.crwa.org/cleanup). Organizations involved are all focused on local and state issues and include the Charles River Watershed

A nation that fails to plan intelligently for the development and protection of its precious waters will be condemned to wither because of its shortsightedness. The hard lessons of history are clear, written on the deserted sands and ruins of once proud civilizations.

—LYNDON B. JOHNSON

Association, Senator Steven Tolman's Office, Charles River Conservancy, the Esplanade Association, the City of Newton, the Trustees of Reservations, Emerald Necklace Conservancy, and the Massachusetts Department of Conservation and Recreation.

The Friends of the Los Angeles River (FoLAR; www.folar.org), a nonprofit organization created in 1986, run an annual cleanup event similar to that in Boston. Since their inception, the organization has had a number of victories in relation to protecting the river. They have helped to create the Cornfield Yards community park along the river, which now occupies a 30-acre piece of land that was originally meant for warehouse development. Their efforts brought together all those who held a stake in the land, such as the Chinatown Yard Alliance, Concerned Citizens of South Central L.A., and the Sierra Club. The state park at Taylor Yard, which occupies the 220-plus acre area of a former railroad yard, was another project of FoLAR, as was the prevention of a 28-foot wall being built for flood protection on the banks of the last 12 miles of the river. Instead of utilizing the wall, the Los Angeles and San Gabriel Rivers Watershed Council was established to discuss the river's future.

Osmosis: *noun*
: the diffusion of fluids through membranes or porous partitions

Although not as well known as the Charles or Los Angeles rivers, the Winooski River in northern Vermont is another important American waterway. As a tributary of Lake Champlain, the Winooski has created a major valley way and flows through the Green Mountains. The local organization Friends of the Winooski (www.winooskiriver.org) has not been faced with major pollution problems, but instead has been able to protect and restore the waterway through recreation and educational activities. Their current projects include monitoring water quality, restoring riparian areas, improving habitats, enhancing access points, and assisting landowners. They also offer guided river paddling trips and walks through the river area that provide both education and enjoyment. Unguided recreational activities such as fishing, boating, and camping are also encouraged as ways to understand and protect the waterway.

GLOBAL EFFORTS FOR CHANGE

Recognizing that the water crisis is being experienced globally, the United Nations has declared the 10 years from 2005 to 2015 to be the International Decade for Action Water for Life. The goal of this decade is to

pH: *noun*
: a numerical measure of the acidity or alkalinity of a solution, usually measured on a scale of 0 to 14; neutral solutions (such as pure water) have a pH of 7, acidic solutions have a pH lower than 7, and alkaline solutions have a pH higher than 7

support the success of international commitments to clean up water and guard its cleanliness for the future. The United Nations also focuses on making clean water available to those in need. Their Millennium Development Goals aim to decrease by half the number of people without access to safe drinking water and to end the exploitation of water resources.

As an ongoing project, no large-scale action has been achieved, although high-level international conferences have been ongoing and various events are being sponsored by the Water for Life campaign. The United Nations has planned a number of public events including seminars, conferences, and expositions for the Water for Life Decade, alongside the annual meetings between international powers to discuss water issues. While most countries have a specific committee appointed to work with the United Nations during this decade, all are invited to participate in the thousands of scheduled public events.

COMMITTING TO CHANGE FOR THE FUTURE

In the United States, legislation has come a long way since the passing of the CWA in the early 1970s. It is true

Reservoir: *noun*
: a natural or artificial place where water is collected and stored for use, especially water for supplying a community, irrigating land, furnishing power, etc.

that the CWA brought about drastic improvements in the country's surface water; pollution sources are now better controlled and there are more organizations and legislation in place to regulate quantity and type of waste being released. However, although the CWA has made it possible for Americans to swim in more lakes and rivers in the 20th century than ever before, the country's problems with pollution aren't over. In September 2009, the *New York Times* published their series Toxic Waters, an investigative report on the pollution of American waterways and the action (or lack thereof) being taken by regulators. This report found that the number of violations of the CWA increased by 16 percent between 2004 and 2007. Furthermore, less than 3 percent of these violations were met with fines or considerable punishment by state officials and the EPA.

The lack of enforcement against such violations is certainly an area in which much improvement should be made in order for the CWA to fulfill its original purpose of guaranteeing a clean water supply. Furthermore, it is up to each one of us to take action to protect the water supply, not just for ourselves, but for every individual on the planet. Elsewhere in the

Spring: *noun*
: an issue of water from the earth, taking the form, on the surface, of a small stream or standing as a pool or small lake

world, involvement on an individual level is also fundamental to bringing about change. The United Nations' international Water for Life campaign requires the participation of individuals around the world and international governing bodies to be a success. Around the world, people everywhere are also encouraged to become involved by working with organizations that have been using the worldwide focus on the subject to energize their own campaigns, as well as to perform simple activities in support of this cause. Some of the 50 activities the United Nations suggests include organizing a "Save Our Water" concert, involving medical students in research, and creating posters or other advertising material to support World Water Day or the entire Water for Life campaign.

YOUR EFFORTS FOR CHANGE

Whether used for agriculture, direct consumption, or manufacturing of goods, the ways in which we use our water are vital to assess the best ways to protect the global water supply for future generations. Although many water issues may seem solvable only through legislation and the work of national and global organi-

Surface Tension: *noun*
: the force exerted along the surface of a fluid that causes it to "bead up" and form into drops; water has high surface tension and beads up easily

zations, there is a level of power available to the people to fight for their access to clean water.

YOUR ROLE
IN ENSURING
A SUSTAINABLE
FUTURE

Taken together, individual small steps can lead to great change. Water is a resource that must be used responsibly. Our actions can also help undo past damage and establish better practices for the future.

ALTHOUGH THE world's freshwater is regularly recycled and replaced through the water cycle, today's population is using the resource faster than it can be replenished.

Every human should have the idea of taking care of the environment, of nature, of water. So using too much or wasting water should have some kind of feeling or sense of concern. Some sort of responsibility and with that, a sense of discipline.

   —THE 14TH DALAI LAMA TENZIN GYATSO

Information about climate change and pollution on our Earth can make the situation seem dire. However, every fact we learn presents an opportunity to act. Rising sea levels and phenomena such as the Trash Vortex are not just disheartening realities; rather, they are a call to make a change. The choices we make today can influence the future and, in this way, each one of us has great power. Even simple actions such as signing a petition or talking with those around you about water issues like the Trash Vortex can help to raise awareness and make an important impact. Guarding a clean water supply and protecting the health of our waterways is a responsibility that falls to each one of us. Making better decisions today will mean a brighter world for us and for future generations.

Big changes are required, but our individual efforts for change are essential. Informing ourselves about water purity levels in our communities and writing to political leaders to demand improvements is vital. Each one of us must play an active role in protecting our planet's water supply for the future as well as for ourselves, and we should begin now by raising our voices for change.

If there is magic on this planet, it is contained in water.
        —LOREN EISELEY

The path towards positive change begins with rethinking our relationship to water and how we use it. Start by adopting a new way of thinking about how you use water every day.

The problem begins at home, but so does the solution. You can make efforts for change.

The first step is to broaden your thinking.

EVALUATE HOW YOU USE WATER

Having continual access to clean water is a luxury in today's world, and maintaining a consistent source of clean water comes with a level of responsibility. Simple actions like taking shorter showers and turning off the faucet while brushing your teeth can help to conserve our water supply. Conserving water may not be the most convenient action to take, but limiting your water usage saves money and energy as well. Your water bill will be less, and less energy will be required to treat water and redistribute it in your community. Reflect on your daily water usage and consider how much water you actually need. Encourage your family, friends, and those in your workplace to look at how

Life originated in the sea, and about eighty percent of it is still there.
—ISAAC ASIMOV

much water they use and whether they too can take action to conserve.

Next, begin to ask questions about your water supply. Where do you get water from? How is the quality and supply? How is wastewater treated?

Then, look beyond what comes out of your faucet to what is in the ground. Are there factories nearby whose industrial waste could pollute your local waterways? Does your town regulate how much and what kinds of waste can be dumped? By making yourself knowledgeable about your local water supply, you can demand stricter regulations and better access to clean water.

THINK ABOUT YOUR COMMUNITY

"Think global, act local." This phrase, originally associated with the ideas of Scottish town planner Patrick Geddes, encourages people to understand the state of the entire planet and to then take action within their own community. Although Geddes didn't use this exact phrase in his writings, his work as a town planner exemplified the application of global ideas at the local

The Waters are Nature's storehouse in which she locks up her wonders.
—Izaak Walton

level. The water crisis is a worldwide issue that occurs in our own towns and cities.

Conserving water helps the environment: the less water used by humans, the more is available to animals and plants. In places like Nevada, Arizona, and other desert regions of the United States, water conservation is no longer an option but a necessity. Local governments have applied restrictions on water usage that limit the amount of water use based on the state of available water supplies. Familiarize yourself with any restrictions your community may have so you can properly follow them when needed. But don't be afraid to become involved in local water activism as well. Within your community you can attend town meetings, write letters to local newspapers, or petition and write to representatives for their support of important water legislation. Also, look for water organizations in your area. Most are eager to take volunteers who can do anything from distributing flyers to helping take water samples or working on restoring a wetland.

KEEP LEARNING

Take an active interest in becoming aware. There are so many important environmental issues about

Water is the lifeblood of our bodies, our
economy, our nation and our well-being.
—STEPHEN JOHNSON

which you can become informed. As you have seen, the problems with availability and access to clean water are numerous and occur all over the globe. Taking an active interest in your personal water use and your community's water system will help ensure this resource is being used sustainably. Part of being responsible about water usage means taking action not only for yourself and your own community, but also implementing long-term change for future generations, all around the world. Make an effort to be informed about issues that extend beyond your community to the greater population.

There are also a number of organizations that have emerged with global access to clean water as their mission.

SIMPLE WAYS TO HELP

Every time you try to build a better habit, you move the entire human race one step closer to ensuring a safe water supply for generations. The world's water crisis may sometimes seem endless, but with great problems come even greater solutions. Here are simple ways that you can help, right now. Begin today.

Water! Blessed water! Everywhere it is a beautiful thing—glistening in the dew drop, dancing in the hail-storm, hanging in ice-drops like jewels on the trees.

    —JOHN BALLANTINE GOUGH

YOUR BUYING POWER

Each purchase we make as consumers is an opportunity to express our support of a company's environmental policies. Furthermore, our decisions as consumers can directly impact the health of the environment by contributing to the conservation of our Earth's precious resources, thereby reducing waste and thus pollution.

Perhaps the most obvious consumer decision we can make is to avoid purchasing bottled water. Although there are times when drinking bottled water is a necessity, making the conscious decision to purchase and use a reusable container instead of bottled water is a simple action we can take as consumers. Buying appliances built to conserve water and energy is a larger commitment, but it is another action we can take.

Your role as a consumer is incredibly important. By making an effort to become educated about the environmental issues, whether through watching the news, scanning the daily headlines, or even just by reading this book, you are becoming an informed consumer who holds the power to impact the environment. Not consuming bottled water and purchasing low-impact appliances are obvious decisions that can

Erosion: *noun*
: the gradual wearing away of land surface materials, especially rocks, sediments, and soils, by the action of water, wind, or a glacier

be made, but as a consumer there are also the opportunities to support those companies whose business practices are aligned with protecting and improving the health of the environment. As a reader, stay informed, take initiative, and use your buying power to support a cleaner and healthier future for Earth.

LIMITING THE USE
OF OUR WATER

In addition to guarding the cleanliness of our water, limiting our use of this finite resource is imperative to guarding our future.

How do we use water? Globally, an average of 8 percent of the global freshwater supply is used for domestic and municipal purposes, 22 percent for industrial activity, and 70 percent for agriculture.

In the United States, we use more water than the rest of the world. The organization charity: water reported that the average American uses 150 gallons of water per day, compared to those in developing countries who are often able to access less than five gallons per day.

Glacier: *noun*
: a slowly moving mass of ice originating from
an accumulation of snow

CONSERVING WATER: HOW TO TAKE ACTION

Together, we can make a difference and reduce water waste. Our efforts for change can begin right in our own backyards. Each day, every one of us can take small steps to conserve our most precious resource.

Here are 11 tips to help ensure a lasting water supply:

Inside your house

1. Make sure your home does not have leaks or dripping faucets.
2. Use automatic dishwashers and washing machines only when there is a full load.
3. When replacing appliances, look for those that are energy efficient. They will save water and reduce your energy bill.
4. Keep a pitcher of water in the refrigerator to avoid running the faucet each time you want a glass of cold water.
5. Install low-flow showerheads to reduce the amount of water used when showering.
6. Install low-flow toilets.

Tributary: *noun*
: a stream that flows into a river, a larger stream, or a lake

Outside your house

7. Grow plants that require less water. This means reevaluating which plants and flowers you choose to landscape your yard. One option is to create a natural habitat garden, which relies on those plants that will grow most easily in the climate of the area where you live.

8. If you have a garden, use drip irrigation instead of sprinklers. If you use sprinklers, adjust their positioning to avoid watering sidewalks and streets.

9. Use rain barrels to collect rainwater and use it to water your plants or wash your car.

10. Recycle the water you use. Learn how to collect *gray water* and use it for gardening, landscaping, or lawn maintenance. (The EPA defines *gray water* as domestic wastewater from kitchen sinks and tubs, clothes, washing machines, and laundry tubs).

11. Sweep your sidewalks and driveways instead of hosing them down.

Levee: *noun*
: a deposit of sand or mud built up along, and sloping away from, either side of the flood plain of a river or stream.

GUARDING THE CLEANLINESS OF OUR WATER

While reducing the amount of water that we waste is important, making sure that our water supplies are kept clean is also vital.

Today, the future of clean water sources is at risk, a crisis that threatens over 100 million Americans. Each one of us must get involved to protect the cleanliness of our water. This is easier than you think. If each one of us would just change a few small habits, we could make a big difference.

GUARDING CLEAN WATER: HOW TO TAKE ACTION

It is up to each one of us to keep our water supplies clean. Simple habits and lifestyle changes make all the difference. Each day, taking small steps to prevent water pollution will lead to big change. We can take action to ensure that our water supplies are clean for future generations.

Cloudburst: *noun*
: a sudden and very heavy rainfall

Here are 10 tips to help ensure a clean water supply:

1. Do not dump any liquids or garbage down storm drains or in rivers, lakes, or streams.
2. Reduce your use of fertilizers.
3. Sweep your gutters and the area in front of your house, including your driveway and sidewalk, free of leaves and other garbage to prevent it from flowing into street drains.
4. Compost your leaves and yard waste.
5. Educate yourself about how to prevent problems with pests without using harsh chemicals. If you do have to use chemical products, choose the least toxic, use the least amount possible, and be sure to follow the label directions.
6. Direct gutters and spouts away from paved surfaces to prevent water from flowing into the street's storm drains. Instead, consider gathering that water for other uses (see number 9 in the previous list about conserving water use outside your home).

Drought: *noun*
: a period of dry weather, especially a long one
that is injurious to crops

7. Rather than wash your car in your driveway, where runoff from soap and other chemicals can flow into storm drains, take your car to the car wash.

8. Check your car regularly for leaks, and always recycle motor oil.

9. When walking your pet outdoors, always clean up after your animal to reduce waste in public places.

10. Be sure to have your septic tank and system inspected on a regular basis.

A BETTER FUTURE

Certain changes must occur on a national or global government level, such as enforcement of the Clean Water Act by the EPA and the support of a global infrastructure that doesn't rely on water privatization. Efforts made on the individual level, however, are equally as important.

In order to continue to have safe, clean drinking water, each one of us must take action to protect it. Water is the basis of our future, and our choices hold the key to guarding our water supply.

AFTERWORD

WATER, IN all its forms, is an amazing resource. It enables life on Earth, from fish and
animals to plants and entire ecosystems. Water is what
makes our own existence possible, and its majestic
lakes, rivers, and oceans nurture our spirit. It is up to
us to preserve this important resource for future generations. We are at a time when we need to confront
the realities as we push ahead. And we must do so
through thought, action, and leadership. There is no
one individual leader for the future. Each of us owns
that role. Therefore, there is open ground for hope and
possibility.

NOTES

Plutarch, *Placita philosophorum*.

INTRODUCTION

Hogan, Linda, *Dwellings: A Spiritual History of the Living World*. (New York: Touchstone, 1995).

United Nations Economic and Social Council, "Comprehensive assessment of the freshwater resources of the world" (presented at the Fifth Session of the Commission on Sustainable Development, April 7–25, 1997).

CHAPTER 1

Walton, Izaak, *The Compleat Angler; or, The Contemplative Man's Recreation*. (London: Chatto & Windus, 1875).

Auden, W.H., "First Things First." *Collected Poems*. (New York: Random House, 2007).

Cousteau, Jacques, http://www.ozh2o.com/h2quotes. html.

CHAPTER 2
Cullney, John L., "Wilderness Conservation," September–October 1990, http://www.ozh2o.com/h2quotes. html.
Borland, Hal, *Sundial of the Seasons*. (Lippincott, 1964).
"Poet of the Depths" *Time*, March 28, 1960. http://www. time.com/time/magazine/article/0,9171,826158-1,00.html

CHAPTER 3
Da Vinci, Leonardo, http://www.ozh2o.com/h2quotes. html.
Thoreau, Henry David, *The Portable Thoreau*. Edited by Carl Bode. (Penguin, 1964).
Gilpin, Laura, *The Rio Grande, River of Destiny*. (New York: Duell, Sloan and Pearce, 1949).

CHAPTER 4
Thoreau, Henry David, *Walden: An Annotated Edition*. Edited by Walter Harding. (Houghton Mifflin Harcourt, 1995).

Saint-Exupery, Antoine de, *Wind, Sand and Stars*. Translated by Lewis Galantière. (Orlando: Harcourt Brace & Company, 1967).

CHAPTER 5

Da Vinci, Leonardo, http://www.ozh2o.com/h2life.html.

Muskie, Edmund S., Speech, March 1, 1966.

United States Geological Survey, "How much water does it take to grow a hamburger?," http://ga2.er.usgs. gov/edu/sc1action.cfm.

United States Geological Survey, "Irrigation water use," http://ga.water.usgs.gov/edu/wuir.html.

Faludi, Jeremy, "Saving the World, Drip by Drip," *WorldChanging*, August 6, 2006. http://www.world changing.com/archives/004787.html.

United States Geological Survey, "Irrigation water use," http://ga.water.usgs.gov/edu/wuir.html.

CHAPTER 6

Reisner, Mark, *Cadillac Desert: The American West and Its Disappearing Water*. (New York: Viking, 1986.

Postel, Sandra, "A Freshwater Expert and Author Answers Questions," *Grist*, April 26, 2004.

Bowden, Charles, *Killing the Hidden Waters*. (Austin: University of Texas Press, 1977).

CHAPTER 7

Clark, William C., Speech, Racine, Wisconsin, April 1988.

World Health Organization, "Water for Health Enshrined as a Human Right," November 27, 2002. http://www.who.int/mediacentre/news/releases/pr91/en/

Environmental Working Group, "A National Assessment of Tap Water Quality: More than 140 contaminants with no enforceable safety limits found in the nation's drinking water," December 20, 2005. http://www.supremedrinkingwatersolutions.com/Tap_Water.html.

United States Geological Survey, "Pharmaceuticals, Hormones, and Other Organic Wastewater Contaminants in U.S. Streams," June 2002. http://toxics.usgs.gov/pubs/FS-027-02/.

Handwerk, Brian, "Giant Ocean-Trash Vortex Documented—A First," *National Geographic News*, September 4, 2009.

CHAPTER 8

Carson, Rachel, *Silent Spring: First Mariner Books Edition*. (New York: Houghton Mifflin Harcourt, 2002).

Nhat Hanh, Thich, *Present Moment Wonderful Moment: Mindfulness Verses for Daily Living*. (Parallax Press, 2006).

Kennedy, John F., "The President's News Conference," April 12, 1961. http://www.presidency.ucsb.edu/ws/index.php?pid=8055.

United States Environmental Protection Agency, "Agriculture and Food Supply," http://www.epa.gov/climate change/effects/agriculture.html.

United Nations Development Programme, "Beyond Scarcity: Power, poverty and the global water crisis," *Human Development Report 2006*. http://hdr.undp.org/en/reports/global/hdr2006/.

Unicef, "Water, Sanitation and Hygiene," July 6, 2010. http://www.unicef.org/wash/.

CHAPTER 9

Franklin, Benjamin, *Poor Richard's Almanack*. (Iowa: The U.S.C. Publishing Company, 1914).

Wright, Jim, "The Coming Water Famine," 1966.

Johnson, Stephen, Speech, 2007.

Water Footprint Network, "Product Water Footprints," http://www.waterfootprint.org/?page=files/product gallery.

State Environmental Resource Center, "Water Privatization Policy Issues Package," http://www.sercon line.org/waterPrivatization/fact.html.

Food and Water Watch, "Water Contaminants? Bottled Water No Help," March 10, 2008. http://www. foodandwaterwatch.org/press/press-releases/water-contaminants-bottled-water-no-help/.

CHAPTER 10

Udall, Stewart, http://www.udall.gov/NewsAnnouncem ents/News/StewartLUdall1920-2010.aspx.

Roosevelt, Franklin D., "A Message to the Congress on the Use of Our National Resources," January 24, 1935. http://newdeal.feri.org/speeches/1935c.htm.

Johnson, Lyndon B., "Letter to the President of the Senate and to the Speaker of the House Transmitting an Assessment of the Nation's Water Resources," November 18, 1968.

United States Environmental Protection Agency, "Biological Indicators of Watershed Health," http://www. epa.gov/bioiweb1/html/biointeg.html.

Charles River Watershed Association, "Annual Earth Day Charles River Cleanup," http://www.crwa.org/ cleanup.html.

Duhigg, Charles, "Clean Water Laws Are Neglected, at a Cost in Suffering," *The New York Times*, September 12, 2009. http://www.nytimes.com/2009/09/13/us/13 water.html?pagewanted=all.

CHAPTER 11

Swanson, Peter, *Water: The Drop of Life.* (Darby: Diane Publishing Company, 2007).

Eiseley, Loren, *The Immense Journey.* (New York: Random House, 1957).

Asimov, Isaac and Jason A. Shulman, *Isaac Asimov's Book of Science and Nature Quotations.* (New York: Grove Press, 1990).

Heyward, Emily, "Charity Water: Making Trade-Offs," *The 99 Percent*, http://the99percent.com/articles/5775/charity-water-making-trade-offs.

AFTERWORD

Gough, John B., *Orations: delivered on various occasions* (W. Tweedie, 1867).

ACKNOWLEDGMENTS

HATHERLEIGH PRESS would like to extend a special thank you to Elizabeth Pacheco and June Eding—without your hard work and dedication this book would not have been possible.

NOTES

NOTES

NOTES